The Artistry of an Artist,
Lorenzo Green

Just in Time for the Hair Salon Guest

Lorenzo Louis Green

ISBN 978-1-63844-045-1 (paperback)
ISBN 978-1-63903-373-7 (hardcover)
ISBN 978-1-63844-046-8 (digital)

Christian Faith Publishing, Inc.
832 Park Avenue
Meadville, PA 16335
www.christianfaithpublishing.com

Printed in the United States of America

A man's gift opens doors for him, and before the great, it gives him access to important people. A man's gift makes room for him.

—Proverbs 18:16

About This Book

This book is for the hairstylist and the hair guest. I want to teach the hairstylist how to get customers, retain customers, and expand your business through retail of hair products. This book is also for the hair guest because you are the most important aspect of the beauty business, and you deserve the best services possible.

Today the beauty industry is a multibillion dollar industry. The entrepreneur who is organized and operates and assumes the risk for business ventures, the market is yours. When the consumer comes to a mall or just decides to go shopping, he or she is looking for the merchant whose product is marketable. I can't over emphasize this.

I remember in the 1990s, I worked in Manassas, Virginia, at Manassas Mall at Regis Hair Salon, and one morning, I opened at 10:00 a.m. and I noticed a lady entering the mall. I didn't pay much attention because it's normal for ladies to park and wait for the mall to open. Now this was my day to close, so around seven thirty that evening, I went down to the food court to get dinner, and whom did I see? It was the same woman who came in when I opened. I said this is unbelievable! She is still here, and so I said to myself, *She is trying to find something else to buy*. I walked up to her and said, "My name is Lorenzo. What's your name?"

She said, "Carolyn."

I said, "I work at Regis Hair Salon, and I would love to do your hair." I touched her on the arm with a little push and said, "I can do it now." She came right along with me. You see, sometimes people need to be told what to do. When I approached the lady, I was dressed professionally and I spoke with confidence. I want to elaborate or, should I say, simplify the four steps to becoming a successful cosmetologist:

1. Come to work ready for work, well groomed, and on time. Don't make the client have to wait on you. She has things to do, people to see, and places to go.
2. Consult with every client. Ask questions about hair maintenance, get their views, and give your views. It's a time when you are up close sometimes for the first time with the client, and fragrance is very important. If you are a smoker, quit. If you can't quit, seek help with getting help. If you choose to continue, after smoking, wash your hands, brush your teeth, put a mint in your mouth, and slightly spray a fragrance on. Smoking has a bad odor. It's offensive and it's poor etiquette.
3. Sell services. Selling services helps you, the stylist, and of course, it helps the client because it's their look that makes the difference. Show that you care. You are changing their look, feeling, and attitude.
4. Promote yourself. Look, act, and dress the part. Be professional always. Give each client three of your business cards. Don't sit back and accept the seasons or say this is the time for business to be slow. There's never a time not to make money. Plan for the upcoming seasons and holidays.

Foreword

Just in Time

This book offers many checks and balances for any hairstylist who wishes to be a successful entrepreneur. In this book, Lorenzo recommends that hairstylists not only use top-of-the-line products like Dudley's products but also retail them. Lorenzo also speaks to how to engage customers in a unique and authentic manner.

He uses Biblical principles in guiding readers to posture themselves in a way that promotes the best quality of service. He does this by using a vibrant metaphor of Christ feeding the multitudes. In this, he exemplifies how a hairdresser can use scarce resources to create wealth and abundance in their businesses.

This a must-read for cosmetologists who want to succeed in this business.

Alfred Dudley Sr.

Mr. Green, the Businessman

1. Mr. Green is writing this book with a purpose.
2. Mr. Green's book not only generates interest but also tells his story.
3. Mr. Green has pinpointed his guests' experiences.
4. Mr. Green's secret is not only his kindness but also his guidance.
5. Mr. Green is laser-focused on his message.
6. Mr. Green personalizes his approach to business.
7. Mr. Green also believes his guests should be entertained.
8. Mr. Green's presentation invites new guests of all ages.
9. Mr. Green's fifty-seven years of experience has been a call to action, which is to satisfy all his guests
10. Mr. Green believes there are simple things that can be done each day to improve his engagement with his guests and team.
11. Mr. Green has created a level of comradery over the years that his guests and team only recognize as good business.

Mr. Sul Allyn

Preface

I view my book to be Christlike when he fed five thousand people with two fish and one loaf of bread. I want my book to be food for the cosmetologist and feed millions who seek knowledge and care. I take to heart the beauty business. I hope with all my heart and hard work that my book will turn the business back to the beauty salon and away from the mom and pop stores. When the client returns, welcome them back to your salon and give them the best service they've ever had.

This book is written with you in mind. To all my readers and guests, I want you to know that this book has been a morning with thoughts, an afternoon with a plan, an evening I'll always remember, and nights with dreams realized. I trust it will be helpful in many ways.

Sincerely,
Lorenzo

Acknowledgement

I want to thank all these salon schools and colleges for giving me the opportunity to work and learn in their salon schools and colleges:

1. Calvinade Beauty Academy, Washington DC
2. Calvinade Beauty Salon, Washington DC
3. Mr. Barnes Hair Salon, Seat Pleasant, Maryland
4. Genesis 1 Hair Salon, Washington DC
5. Mr. Wilson Hair Salon, Washington DC
6. Johnson Product Co., Makers of Ultra Sheer & Afro Sheen
7. Mizani Product Co. Classes
8. Paul Mitchell Advance School
9. Influence Product Co. Classes
10. Botugen Hair System
11. Dudley Advance College, North Carolina
12. Ollie Benson Hair Cutting Class, Boston, Massachusetts
13. Hair Designer Plus, Hyattsville, Maryland
14. Joe's Hair Salon, Culpepper, Virginia
15. New York Hair Fashion, Washington DC
16. Hair Cuttery, Culpepper, Virginia
17. Regis Hair Salon, Manassas, Virginia
18. Seoul Hair Design, Beltsville, Maryland
19. Pat's Hair Care, Beltsville, Maryland
20. Renew Hair, Beltsville, Maryland

Over fifty-seven years of knowledge care and love.

What a gratifying day I had on April 10, 2019. My instructor from Beauty School in 1967 came to the salon to get hair service here at the Hair Cuttery in Bowie, Maryland. I've been doing her hair since beauty school over fifty-one years ago.

I introduced her to my district manager and team leader.

That occasion was coincidental for my book but right on time.

One of the most important services of the beauty salon business is customer service. You see, customer service is like filling a prescription. It's the act of taking care of the guests' needs by providing and delivering professional, helpful, high-quality services and assistance before, during, and after the guest requirements are met. Customer service is the support you offer your guest—both before and after they buy and use products or services. Make sure they have an enjoyable experience. Always compliment your guest during hair services. With rising costs, your money gets lost. Sell six retails a day and make extra pay.

Introduction

I grew up in the country. I'm talking about real country. We lived in a four-room, two-family house—two rooms for us and two rooms for the other family. My sister, Priscilla, and my brother, Robert, we slept in the kitchen on folding carts. We had a wood stove in the kitchen, a table and a barrel shaped Maytag washing machine. My mom and dad slept in the living room. We were poor and happy. We didn't know we were poor because my mom and dad made sure we looked good and clean. We wore used clothing, but we always looked sharp like my picture on the poster! You see my Windsor necktie knot!

We lived steps away from the Memorial Baptist Church where my mom and dad sang in the choir. I couldn't wait to get home after church to play ball. I would go right to the front yard to play ball, but my dad would say, "Go around back and play. You know today is Sunday."

I would say, "Daddy, it's Sunday in the backyard too." We lived like that for about three years, and then we moved on to stay with my uncle because he needed us to help him. We raised cattle, pigs, and horses. I always wanted to make my own money, so I would walk the railroad track and pick up coals that fell off the train and brought them back in town and sold them for five cents. It was a luxury to burn coals for heat.

You are only four steps away from success.

1. Come to work.
2. Consult with every client.
3. Sell services.
4. Promote yourself.

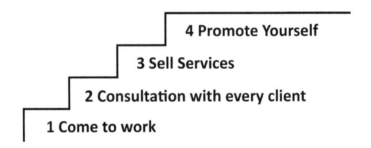

4 Promote Yourself

3 Sell Services

2 Consultation with every client

1 Come to work

Beauty School

My classmates laugh at me because I would burn customers' ears or color the hair the wrong color, like I remember not paying attention and picking up the wrong bottle. The customer's hair was blond. She needed a touch-up. I picked up black. It took me all day to bleach it back to blond. During the 1960s and 1970s, teasing was in. I teased this lady's hair so high she had to bend her head down to get out the front door. I was determined to learn. Another time I had to curl this lady's hair, and it took me all day.

After about eight months in school, I entered a competition hair show and won first place and second place. I was very excited about being in school. I would ask my family to let me do their hair. While in the Navy, I met this young lady, which I later married, but while we were dating, I asked her to come to the school one day so I could show her off to my classmates. I shampooed, cut, and styled her hair, and after doing all of that, she combed the style out right in front of my classmates. I've never been so hurt in all my days.

That took me back to the days when I was in the Navy and I first met her in Portsmouth, Virginia. I walked up. She was standing on the porch and seemed to be a nice young lady. I had just purchased a bottle of Hogshead Wine. I hid the wine behind my back so she wouldn't see it. After that incident, I wished I had drunk the wine. We are divorced now.

After graduating from Calvinade Beauty School, I worked at Calvinade Hair Salon. The director was always fond of me because of how I succeeded. I learned the business of the industry. I love the business of business; it's making money. Let me pause and tell you about one of my childhood fantasies of Christmas toys that I never did get. It would fascinate me the steps in operating a cash register. How you can just push a button, a bell would ring, and money would jump out! I look back to now, fifty-seven years later, and this is why I love the art of the business.

Although this book is about making money in the beauty business, I wrote it to hopefully save you money and thousands of miles in travelling to conventions and classes. Also, I wrote this book using biblical principles to help you become the best cosmetologist and the greatest salesperson possible. Do you know who the greatest salesperson in the world is? Some would consider him the founder of modern business. Who do you know could attract and retain twelve ordinary men from the lower class of society and, through mentorship, motivation, and empowerment, help them become extraordinary men in an awesome organization that gained victory over this world?

The answer is, of course, Jesus Christ. In the early part of Jesus's life, he was a carpenter. Then after he was baptized by John the Baptist, he became a fisher of men—twelve disciples to be exact. Not only that, he said to those disciples, "Follow me, and I will make you fishers of men" (Matthew 4:19).

In other words, he trained his disciples to emulate him by recruiting others. The Bible says, "But thanks be to God! He gives us the victory through our Lord Jesus Christ" (1 Corinthians 15:57). Jesus Christ also said, "I have told you these things, so that in me you may have peace. In this world, you will have trouble. But take heart! I have overcome the world" (John 16:33).

Jesus kept things real, acknowledging that we will have trouble; however, don't give up. He will show us how to overcome the world. All we must do is follow Him.

As I said above, it is my intent in writing this book to use biblical principles. Jesus fed five thousand people with five loaves of bread and two fish. He said,

> They need not depart; give ye them to eat. He said, "Bring them hither to me." And he commanded the multitude to sit down on the grass, and took the five loaves, and the two fish, and looking up to heaven, he blessed, and brake the loaves to his disciples, and the disciples to the multitude. And they did all eat and were filled: and they took up of the fragments that remained twelve baskets full. And they that had eaten were about five thousand men, beside women and children. (Matthew 14:17–21)

Someone said that success is a road always under construction. Success is a journey, never a destination. However, there are keys to success: planning, setting short-range and long-range objectives. One of the key things you must know: how much a customer is worth to you.

Cosmetology is a service profession and a loving profession. True to the notion, what the mind can conceive, you can achieve. You need to have the burning desire to be successful. Don't let pride get in the way. Ask your customer to help you. Give each customer three business cards and say to them, "Please tell your family and friends about me." Remember what Jesus said to his disciples. Ask and it shall be given. Seek and you will find. Knock and the door will open.

In human relations, first a person must develop skills because we deal with a variety of individuals. Since being in a people business and the better you are with yourself and people, the more profitable your business is going to be. You are going to be on time and not waste the clients' time. Time is one of life's great virtues. A time-conscious person is highly respected and admired. Clients place trust, hope, and admiration in stylists who are always conscious of time. How much is your time worth to you? Value your time and your clients. Learn to work on holidays as a successful person in business do, and over time, you will build and add years to your work life. Some people are time-oriented; other people are event-oriented. Enjoy what you do. Make fun out of it like a game. Admire, love, adore, and cherish what you want. You must give. Be grateful for each customer. Attitude and gratitude can make you successful. The Bible says that if you are grateful over a few, I'll make you master over plenty. You can't ever get angry at the customer; the customer is always king. The business is two words: sale and service.

Before I opened my first salon, I worked very hard on 50 percent commission, staying professional at all times, always promoting, passing out business cards, and increasing my clientele. My clientele grew so big I had to move on to a booth rental—one chair. I outgrew that to two chairs needing a shampoo person. Right today, by you reading my book, it will help you turn the corner. It can start today.

I don't belittle dreamers because I know that he who never dreamed never had a dream to come true. Do your thing, and do it very well, but be mindful that the unemployment offices are full of those who only did their thing. In 1980, I went to night school to get my instructor's license. Right up the street, there was this unisex salon. This hairdresser was sitting on the porch. He said to me, "I don't know why you are leaving your salon going to night school." Never let anyone steal your dreams because he is sitting on the porch today.

Ladies and gentlemen, I want you to know the care you should be getting when you visit the hair salon. Question the hairdresser about continuous use of softener products like balsam and never giving you a protein treatment to stop breakage. Hair is 97 percent protein and 3 percent keratin. Once again, this is time for you to ask that hairdresser, "Have you read Lorenzo's book, *Just in Time for the Hair Salon Guest*? Because it's your look that makes the difference, and I care!"

Your hair has three layers: the cortex, the cuticle, and the medulla. The layers are like fish scales. Whenever chemicals are used, the layers open up. You should apply a bonding neutralizer to close the layer. Leave the bonding on for five minutes. Do not comb and then rinse and proceed with a regular shampoo and conditioner. Some stylists abuse guests, leaving conditioner in longer than twenty to twenty-five minutes.

One time, I saw this lady was under the dryer for one hour. Sometimes guests are scared because they feel the stylist will not give a good hairdo. This is why I'm writing this book. It's been bad for the business. It makes the client stop coming. She'll tell her friends and family about the services. The guest will start doing her own hair. Hair cutting is the backbone of my success and also hair coloring. I love the art of haircutting. It's the base of the style, and trimming the hair ends keeps hair healthy and promotes hair growth. Trimming the hair ends is like pruning a fruit tree to bear more fruit.

Hair Care

Ask your hairdresser about a bonding reform neutralizer. It immediately replenishes the hair with essential conditioners and moisturizers (plant-source proteins and natural humectants). It closes the cuticle and helps to reform the bonds that are broken due to chemical processing. This conditioner injects the hair with vital nutrients that lubricate the hair shaft and restores the balance of moisture. Ask your hairdresser about Dudley's DRC28. It's a deep-penetrating advance hair treatment and fortifier that is concentrated with most of the hairs own natural proteins and amino acids. This rich formula works from the inside out—nourishing, restoring, and repairing severely damaged or weakened hair to stronger, healthier state. Also, Dudley's Cream Protein Hair Conditioner is a moisturizer that strengthens, softens, and restores moisture in the hair shaft. Its rich emollients and hydrolyzed proteins bond to the hair to smooth roughen cuticle layers, reduce tangles, and leave hair with incredible softness and sheen. To you, my guest, I want you to know because your hair needs the care of these products.

Ladies say that a man has a growing hand. That's because he handles the head a little rougher than a lady. Stimulating the blood causes it to circulate and helps the hair to grow. Shampooing is where you win the guest. It's a good feeling. To tell you the truth, I have guests that I've been doing their hair for over fifty years. One of my guests told me that if we were married, we wouldn't have to have sex, just shampoo her hair.

When you read some of the letters that guests wrote as a testament about my profound care, you will begin to understand my personalized approach.

In this business, you should never stop learning. There's always something you can learn to make the stay for your guest comfortable, relaxed, and pleasant. We are losing business to foreigners because we stop learning and not being serious about our business, and they are taking over. The only business they are not taking over is the church. Isn't that a blessing?

Now I must share this with you. At my hair salon in Washington DC, Lorenzo's of Halifax Hair Designers, I almost lost my life from cutting a young man's hair. He said I cut his hair too short and went home and brought his mother back. She walked in the salon and asked, "Who's Lorenzo?"

I said, "That's me."

She said, "Why did you cut my son's hair too short?"

I said, "Miss—"

She pulled out a gun and said, "You are a dead mother. Shut your mouth."

I ran out of the salon so fast, and I didn't look back. It was a scary time. Another time, I cut a client's hair too short, and she complained, went home, told her husband, and brought him back. He liked the cut so well that he asked me to cut his hair. Some you please, and some you don't.

Hair Cuttery

A no-nonsense business. Ms. Shelia said to me, "I've watched you since you've been here, and I knew you would please me." I told her that this was a structure business. She said, "That's what we want." She also mentioned my niece McKeny. I asked her to come here and work. It's a structured business continuing education and an environment that's conducive for artistry. To my colleagues, our guests want and need us to listen to them. I am still cutting my instructor's hair since 1967 at Calvinade Beauty Academy, 1340 H. Street, Northeast, Washington DC. Be honest in what you do and say. After being retired for three years, I decided to get back doing what I love—that's hairdressing. Stylists need to look like the business. You either look like somebody or everybody.

Finally, after going through the morning dew, the noonday, and now it's the sunset of the eve, I'm enjoying the business more than ever. Working at the Hair Cuttery is a joy—total joy. Whether it's styling hair or making sure the salon is clean for the guests, it is a joy. I wake up waiting for the alarm to go off. The music is calm, the stylists are always about the work, and promotion and advertising are always on the BOGO!

Research suggests that the sun helps provide you with nutrients your body needs to sustain a complete hair growth cycle. While your body naturally produces vitamin D when you're in the sun, UV rays are also a major cause of melanoma and other skin cancer. Sunlight allows your body to produce vitamin D, and this, in turn, stimulates the growth of your hair and prevents hair loss. Get out a little more, and let your body receive the vitamins it needs to give you healthy skin and hair. Revel in God's sunshine and embrace its warmth! It turns out human hair does indeed grow faster during summer but only about 10 percent in comparison to hair growth during the winter months. Seasonal changes bring about change in human hair growth. Throughout my career, a lot of my guests would say to me, *Stylist love to cut your hair.* In some cases, that's true because we know the benefits it'll be for your hair. "Cutting the ends of your hair doesn't affect the follicles in your scalp, which determines how fast and how much your hair grows," says Paradi Mirmirani, MD, Assistant Professor of Dermatology at the University of California, San Francisco.

School and Now

I've heard over the years it's in the brand name. I take my name to be a brand name, so let me take you all the way back to when I was growing up in the country. My home is Halifax County, Virginia. When I was a little boy, I didn't like my first name because it sounded country. I would use my middle name, Louis. Everyone would call me Louis Green.

After getting out of the Navy and going to cosmetology school, the director called me Mr. Green, and so did my classmates. After graduating from beauty school, my brand name was Mr. Green for years. I used that name. Later I opened my own salon and named it Lorenzo's of Halifax Hair Designers. It was located at 3916 12th Street, Northeast, in Washington DC. Twenty and a half years passed, and my brother-in-law and I went into business opening a salon, and we named it Hair Designers Plus. I managed it, and there my brand name was Lorenzo. The shop continued for years. Now I'm here at the Hair Cuttery, and I've taken on another brand name: Mr. Lorenzo and Lorenzo. Some of my longtime friends and guests call me Green and Louis. Please continue to call, and I'll take good care of your hair. The Word says a good name is better to be chosen than silver or gold. I have a good name.

My Son's Tomorrow Depends

New Horizons has been supporting Jonathan for over twelve years and offer individuals with intellectual and developmental disabilities to lead productive, fulfilling lives since 1969.

In 1981, my son Jonathan was born with spina bifida. Spina bifida is a type of birth defect called a neural tube defect. It occurs when the bones of the spine (vertebrae) doesn't form properly around part of the baby's spinal cord, and this left Jonathan paralyzed from the waist down. I knew I had work to do. I didn't want him to feel inferior because he was in a wheelchair, as I knew that walking was no big deal. A lot of people are walking, but they're going nowhere. You see, once my son could see that I loved him and cared for him, it gave him confidence about being in a wheelchair. Jonathan's way of getting around is by using his elbows to pull his body forward.

Upon My Today

Jonathan's mother wanted the pastor to pray he would walk, and the pastor did just that. The pastor also told Jonathan that he would be walking by Christmas. I taught Jonathan how to use his elbows to go upstairs. One day, we got three steps from the top of the staircase and Jonathan said, "Who-wee, I'll be glad when Christmas comes." We laughed. Another time, he was on the floor, and my grandson Kevin was crawling around like Jonathan. Jonathan said to me, "Look at Kevin. He wants to be paralyzed like me. Isn't that something, Dad?"

God is merciful and caring, and I am pleased with my son. He painted the artwork on the cover of this card in 2001 and named it, "Lord Have Mercy." Jonathan is an abstract artist.

Abstract Painting by Jonathan

Oh, what a joy it is you being my son. It's an early morning wake up. It's a good night sleep. It's an all-day joy you being my son. You never complain or frown. You're always the same from sunup to sundown. Your sense for style, your pleasant smile, your obedience and belief in Christ will give you eternal life. Continue to stay focused and give life your best. The steps you are taking are the steps to success. My prayers at night, I ask God to protect you from hurt, harm, and danger to me. You're God's little angel. So if I should die and leave you behind, my love is shown for you in this poem on every line.

My poem was well received by President Obama and First Lady Michelle Obama.

Tomorrow

Tomorrow, tomorrow, tomorrow, when will i see tomorrow? Yesterday is just like today, another life has been taken away.

I read about it, it's on TV,
People are crying, expressing their sympathy.
Our Father, which art in Heaven,

Bless the little children,
Some don't live to be eleven.
I went to a wake at a neighborhood funeral parlor,
The deceased friends were from street people to blue collar.

The cause of death was from a drug overdose.
In the next room, another corpse lay
from what do you suppose.
Now killing by handguns hasn't just begun,
And looking at the escalating numbers of deaths,
it seems as though they're killing for fun.

But it's all about drugs and love affairs,
Please, we need more family prayer.
As I sat looking out of my window, in a funny kind of daze,
Thoughts begin to run through my mind about the late
Dr. Martin Luther King's dream and how
it's vanishing in many ways.
I do believe that this corruption will someday come to an end,
When all of God's children will be without sin. I read
it in the Bible, between Genesis and Revelation, That
God didn't want this to happen to his creation.

A tomorrow with the rising of the sun.

A tomorrow when you and I will be called one by one.
A tomorrow when Dr. Martin Luther
King's dream will be a reality.
A tomorrow when justice will run through
every valley, village, and street.
A tomorrow when every man and every woman
will live up to his or her responsibility.

A tomorrow when the color of the skin
no longer decides a man's destiny.
No man is an island, and no man stands alone
Let not your heart be troubled God has
prepared a Heavenly home.
A home where there is no more problems
and difficult situations.
A home where there is a holy spiritual population
Tomorrow, tomorrow, tomorrow when will we see a tomorrow.

By Lorenzo Green
Poet-Orator
1983
Registration Number TXu 1-769-545
Effective date of registration:
August 8, 2011

What a gratifying feeling.

THE WHITE HOUSE
WASHINGTON

Please accept our thanks for your thoughtful gift. We are moved by your generosity.

Your gesture serves as a reminder of the kindness of the American people, and we are grateful for your support of our shared vision for our Nation's future.

Thank you, again, for your gift. We wish you all the best.

Sincerely,

Michelle Obama

My First Place Trophy in Beauty School

1967
Calvinade Beauty School
Lorenzo's Model—Lou Young

Letters of Satisfaction from Guests that
were Happy with the Services

My name is Gabrielle Smith, and I can remember it like yesterday. It was a typical Saturday morning, and I was up early doing my usual Saturday errands. I had just completed my grocery shopping and decided to go to the bank. As I was waiting in line, a gentleman approached me and handed me his business card. I thought, *Oh God, what is he trying to sell so early in the morning?* As he handed me his business card, he said, "I am a stylist and would love to do your hair." Of course, the first thing that entered my mind was, I must look pretty awful for someone to approach me with his business card asking if they could do my hair. Curiously, I asked, "Do I look that bad?"

He said, "No, I just enjoy doing hair, and it would be a pleasure to do yours." No one has ever said that to me before.

He then explained that he has his own hair salon and told me where it was located.

Normally, I would travel to North Carolina to get my hair done. I have an aunt that is a stylist, and she has been the only person that I felt comfortable to do my hair. Ladies, we can all testify that we do not just let anyone do our hair. We consider our hair crowning glory, and we take pride when we walk out of our homes to face the world. Since you only have one time to make a first impression, we make sure we do it with flair and grace.

As the weeks passed, I was in desperate need of a haircut so I decided to go to Mr. Green's shop, Hair Designer's Plus, to see if he would be available to at least talk to me about my hair and possibly make an appointment. Upon entering his salon, the first thing I noticed was how clean and inviting it was. I was also impressed by the type of music that was playing. It's not often you hear spiritual music in a salon. I instantly felt relaxed and at ease. I was able to schedule an appointment for later in that week. When I arrived for my scheduled appointment, I had the opportunity to meet the other stylists. They were very polite, talented, and courteous to all the customers that entered the salon. They all made you feel that it is a pleasure to make sure you are satisfied when you leave the salon.

I have been living in Washington DC for over twenty years and have been to many salons and have had many stylists. Some I have been satisfied with, some, well, let's just say, I do not go to them anymore. But I am happy to admit that I am scheduled for my six-week hair appointment tomorrow and can't wait for Mr. Green to work his magic!

*****

February 1, 2007

Hair Designers Plus
6211 Belcrest Road
Suite #7
Hyattsville, Maryland 20782

Dear Sir/Madam:

I am writing this letter to express my satisfaction to the owner, Mr. Lorenzo L. Green, for the quality of work and customer service of all the staff at Hair Designers Plus.

As a regular customer for a period of eight months, I have been truly impressed with the level of comfort I experience at Hair Designer Plus. The decor of the salon is tasteful, and it is always clean. There is a touch of elegance about it in every aspect including the music. Patrons are always treated with the same courtesy and respect whether they are first timers, walk-ins or regulars. The stylists do excellent work and seldom keep their clients waiting long periods of time. It is refreshing to be in an environment where the staff are well-mannered and do not openly gossip or use offensive language.

It is evident that Mr. Green values all of his clients equally and, in doing so, has considered the comfort of every potential customer as he envisioned the type of person he wanted to attract. And like a true entrepreneur, he is constantly thinking of new ways to improve service. It is a pleasure and rare treat to enter a Black hair salon where the customer is valued and catered to.

I commend Mr. Lorenzo Green for his successful establishment and invite all women looking for an elegant experience in total hair care to visit Hair Designers Plus.

Sincerely,

Deborah Scott Tyson

*****

August 22, 2019

I would like to speak on my experience with one of the best hairstylists I have ever had the pleasure of having an appointment with. First of all, he gives his undivided attention to you. Whatever time your appointment is, he belongs to you and only you. He pays attention to what you ask for. The man is magnificent, very professional all the time. When you are in his presence, nothing matters but the client. He is a psychologist. He listens and he takes his time, no rushing. I have never left not happy with what he has given me. Gentle and strong and a wonderful father. As long as he is doing hair, I will be a customer for life. Not only is he the best hairstylist I have ever had, but he is also my friend for life.

Kathy

I've Always Been On... the Grow
Searching for Success

Lorenzo of Halifax Hair Designers
Owned by Lorenzo Green
3916 12th Street, NE, Washington DC
1980-1993

These are some of my models at a hair show extravaganza that I put on for a fundraiser to generate some money to buy a wheelchair lift to put on my van for my son. The show was held at the Knights of Columbus in Crofton, Maryland. I made flyers to pass out promoting the hair show.

This particular Sunday, I went to church at the Rhema Christian Center, 1825 Michigan Avenue, Northeast with the Pastor Arvel Givens. I asked him if I could pass out flyers after church to raise money to buy the wheelchair lift. He said, "Yes, but ask my mother," which I did, and she said yes. Then he asked me how much does the lift cost? I said $7,395. He said to come Monday, "and I will write you a check."

I went there Monday for afternoon prayer. He called me into his office and wrote the check for $8,000 and said, "You and your son go and have a good lunch." He said, "I have watched you over the years, and you have been faithful with your son." I thanked him and thanked him.

You see, Pastor Arvel knows about my faithfulness to my son who is thirty-seven years old now. Twenty-five years ago, my son was at children's hospital in Washington DC because of a VP Shut Failure. He was in intensive care, and the head doctor in spina bifida, Dr. Sheryl, said to my son's mother that she didn't think he would live through the night. And when she turned to say the same thing to me, I told her I didn't want to hear it. "Don't tell me you are giving up on my son. I'm going home to take a shower, and when I come back, nothing better not happen to my son."

I called this stylist Valerie Anderson, who used to work at my salon, Lorenzo's of Halifax, and she said, "Lorenzo don't worry. Jon is going to be all right." Thanks. Today Jonathan is all right. In life, God will put angels in your path. All you have to do is do the right thing, and nothing but good will happen. The same is true with servicing your guest—do the right thing, don't intimidate your guest.

My Story A

At my son's day program, New Horizons Supported Services for Individuals with Disabilities, they would go out in the community to integrate with the general public. This particular day, they went to Watkins Park in Upper Marlboro, Maryland. I would go with them because Jonathan needed to be catheterized at noon. After I catheterized him, we gathered at the picnic table for lunch. Out of the blue, this squirrel showed up and frightened my son and me, so I looked around for a stick to scare it away.

Behind the table was a pile of branches. I pulled one out and broke it off to chase the squirrel away. After doing so, I looked at the branch and said, "I can do something with this and I did." That started my Walking N' Jogging stick business.

Throughout my book, I mention the road to success is always under construction. In 1997, I worked at Regis Hair Salon in Manassas at Manassas Mall. My hours were from 10:00 a.m. to 5:00 p.m. When I got off, I would go around the corner to Ruby Tuesdays where I worked as a waiter till 9:00 pm.

I had an old Dodge. The heater in the car didn't work, and the temperature was 20 degrees outside that day. I lived in Culpepper, Virginia, a forty-five-minute drive. My hands were so cold. I would put one hand under my armpit to get warm and then switch it with the other. I did what I had to do so that I could pay my bills. I held on to God's unchanging hand and didn't give up.

Today I'm driving a $75,000 Honda Odyssey VMI with automatic heat and air control.

Thanks to God Almighty.

Throughout my book, you'll read about facts, testimonies, and experiences during my career. This testimony is one of me being obedient. In 1996, on a Sunday evening at Rhema Christian Center located at 1825 Michigan Avenue, Northeast, Washington DC, it was communion night, and a spiritual exchange presided by the late Bishop Givens. It was a very special time for me because the next day, which was Monday, I had a court day in Prince William County. Mrs. Jones v. Lorenzo Green.

I was being sued for $250,000 because Mrs. Jones said that she lost hair with a color and curl service that I performed at this salon I worked at. So during the communion ceremony, when the bishop passed out the bread, he said, "If there is anything you want to claim, do it now." I did. I asked God to intervene in my court case the next day.

The next day, I dressed in business attire. I left early so that I wouldn't be late. It was about a forty-five-minute drive from DC. I took the 66 Route, and while driving, I started to sing, "Thank you, Jesus. Thank you, Lord. Thank you, Jesus. Thank you, Lord." And I started crying and then I stopped. I turned onto Route 234 toward the courthouse. I parked in the visitor parking and went inside. I saw the information desk and asked what floor the case Lorenzo Green v. Mrs. Jones was. The guard told me to take the elevator to the second floor. I took the elevator to the second floor, and when I stepped off, the attorney representing the salon walked up to me and said, "Mr. Green, I have good news for you. The case is no longer against you. It is against the salon."

I said, "Oh my god, you are right on time."

The attorney said he just wanted me to stick around to listen to the case. I did and they lost. What a powerful God I serve. I had the almighty attorney representing me, and he has never lost a case.

Celebrity Page

I'll never forget about the time I had the privilege to cut Marvin Gaye's hair. We lived at 1411 Varnum Street, NW Washington DC, and Marvin's family lived on the corner of Varnum and Webster Street. Marvin's mother and my mother were good neighbors, and my dad and Marvin's dad chatted from time to time. Sometimes I would be coming in, and I would see Mr. Gaye raking leaves or doing something outside.

My mother was good for promoting me, and my mother told Mrs. Gaye that I was a hairdresser and barber. This particular day, Mrs. Gaye called my mother and told her that Marvin was in town and if I could come up and cut his hair. When I came in, my mother said to me that Marvin wanted me to cut his hair. I said yes. I was really excited. I grabbed my barbering kit and went up to the house. I introduced myself and said thanks for the phone call. I cut Marvin's hair in the kitchen. We chatted about him being an entertainer, about my career as a hairdresser, and my Navy travels. After I finished cutting his hair, he went in the living room and played the piano. He played two or three songs, and then he went on the front porch and autographed dollar bills and gave them to the kids in the neighborhood. I can remember just like it was yesterday. Every time I hear his music, I think about it.

There was another celebrity, Biz Markie, whose hair I also had the privilege of cutting. This is how I met Biz Markie: I was on my way back to DC from being in New York City at the International Hair Show. Back in the '80s, hairdressers from all over the world showed off their artistry, and at that show, a very good friend of mine, Barry Fletcher, won a Rolls-Royce in a competitive hair performance. I stopped on the New Jersey Turnpike at a diner for a bite to eat.

I'm always passing out my cards. That's how I met Biz Markie. I told him I just left the show and that I was from DC, and I was the owner of Lorenzo's of Halifax Hair Designs. He said he was from the area and would stop by, and he did. When the neighborhood heard that Biz Markie was at my salon, it was standing room only. And his popular song was "Hot Oh Baby You-oo Got What I Need and they say he's just a friend." And I'll never forget that encounter. He had about sixteen pagers on him. I could not believe it. He was very popular. Pagers were going off one after the other.

Now I never thought after fifty-eight years of standing behind the chair and going strong, I'll be as happy as can be. These are my most enjoyable days. Today was Thursday, August 29, 2019, around 9:45 a.m., and a guest just said to me, "I'm going to make sure I get to the salon early because Lorenzo is going to be busy."

My team leader said to me, "How long will it be before you can take someone else?" I'm writing this because I've been busy throughout my career. As I look back, the beginning was challenging, inquisitive, and quite interesting. I want to thank my team leader and Dennis Ratner, CEO, founder, and salon professional, for giving me the opportunity to work in a structural salon with well-trained team leaders and salon professionals—an atmosphere that is conductive for hair artistry, always continuing education.

My profound feeling and thoughts are that Hair Cuttery should be a boot camp for salon professionals. You will never go wrong working at the Hair Cuttery. The owners of Hair Cuttery also own a radio station which plays very soothing music that relaxes the guests. The music also frees the professional stylist's mind and encourages them to think, be creative at work and enjoy the experience while focusing on the guest.

The radio also is a means of education and communication. Expert salon professionals are telling the guest about products and services while we are servicing the guest. Also, it tells the guest about products that they can take home for home maintenance care. So I say to the guest that has already experienced the Hair Cuttery, "Please tell your family and friends."

Now to the sales professionals, I'll share with you, it's a multilevel commission structural business. If you are a goal-setter, business-minded person, it's the salon for you. Tomorrow only belongs to those who prepare for it. It's coming. Where are you going to be when it gets here?

Finally, I was ecstatic when my team leader, Ms. Shayla, told me that my son's day program guest from New Horizons will receive $5 beauty bucks off total hair care services on Wednesday. I couldn't wait to tell Tiasony "Tia" Bazemore, associate director Day Programs.

October 20, 2015

To Friendly Faces Barbers/Stylists:

This is a follow-up reminder for you when the clients enter: friendly faces, ask, "How may I help you?" Do not discuss services. Escort the client to your chair and proceed with a consultation. At the end of the services, it's very simple. It's called a one-liner. Choose a line or sentence from the back of the product and tell the client what it does. Remember, if you use it, they'll choose it.

From,
Lorenzo's Professional Hair Care Concept

Lorenzo's Professional Hair Salon Concept

"This concept will increase your sales by over 55 percent."

Stylists have never been taught this concept: haircuts, relaxer, perms and color. With this concept, I'll show you how to take the fear out of selling and teach you how to sell services to guests. Children's Hospital calls it triage. An adult hospital calls it vital signs. No service or treatment ever starts without it first. *It's the act or procedure of consulting to give expert advice as professionals.*

A few years ago, a guest said to me, "Lorenzo, I've never had a consultant before services."

I'll show you the importance of the following areas:

- Salon
- Waiting
- Reception
- Shampoo
- Styling

I'll teach you the four steps to success. I'll demonstrate how retailing products for home maintenance is as easy as taking candy from a baby. If you are a salon owner with five or more commission stylists, your salon should be making $5,000 or more a month. If you are an independent stylist with this concept, you should make $900 or more a month.

To inquire about more information for your salon or school, contact senior cosmetologist, Lorenzo Green, at 240-463-2167. Lorenzo has over forty-six years of combined experience as a salon owner and senior cosmetologist.

Quotes

"Success usually comes to those who are too busy looking for it."

"Change is a must."

"Once you make a change, never go back."

"Your past does not equal your future."

"Never accept a situation. Do something about it."

My Oldest Daughter's Book Ending Truths

My sister, Dana, and I are truly blessed to have been a part of my dad's legacy. He's a professional entrepreneur and a senior cosmetologist. We have had awesome experiences with our dad who has been manager/owner of two well-known, incredible hair salons in the Washington DC, Maryland, and Virginia area, where my sister and I developed our own clientele. We've had the honor and privilege of assisting my dad with putting together some dynamic hair shows and fundraisers. But the biggest of them all is when Glynn Jackson, the creator and founder of the acclaimed award Golden Scissors Hair Show, stopped by our salon and asked us to enter our stylist into the competition.

The Golden Scissors Hair Show features the excellence and talent of many stylist and barbers. And the icing on the cake was when Phil Cull and Debra Smith from TV One stopped by the salon and spoke with me, my sister, Dana, and my dad about participating with the Golden Scissor Hair Show. They were very inspired to see how family oriented we were with each other and our stylist. Once Phil and Debra sat down and talked to us, we were asked to take part in the TV One documentary titled *Tangles and Locks*, which still airs today. The documentary showed behind-the-scene raw footage of us preparing for the show—the good and the bad. This is no doubt an awesome and memorable experience.

Lynn Green

Senior Cosmetologist, Author,
Poet, Orator, and Artist

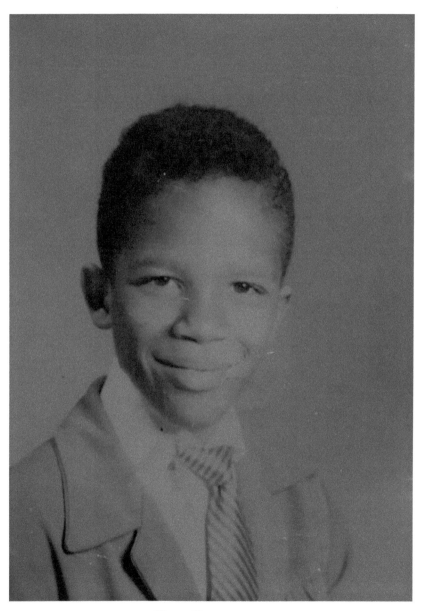

Young Entrepreneur
1952

Navy Barber
1962

Beauty School Winner
(Lorenzo with Lou Francis)
1967

Business card with Dana, Conti, and Patrice

Hair Show Flyer

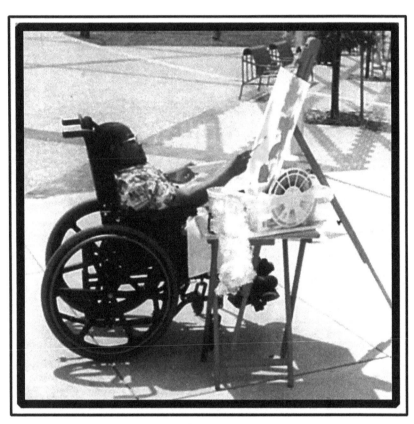

Jonathan painting

"Lord Have Mercy"

Jonathan's painting

Styles by the Dexterous Artist

Lorenzo with Roslyn
Over 20 years Guest/Model

Judy
Over 40 years Guest/Model

Sandy
Over 20 years Guest/Model

Valerie
Former Stylist/Model/Salon Owner

About the Author

Lorenzo Louis Green was born on September 23, 1942, in South Boston, Virginia, to Henry Louis and the late Marion Henderson Green. He is the second son of six children. He was baptized at an early age and became a devoted Christian and lifelong student of the Bible. He attended Mary Bethune High School, and after high school, like his older brother, Robert, Lorenzo served in the US Navy from 1962 to 1966 as a ship serviceman barber with the ranking of E3. After being discharged from the Navy honorably, he wanted to be a DC policeman; however, his father suggested that he go to school for cosmetology to build on his skills in barbering.

It is very hard writing this part. It happened on November the 13, 1963, on an evening after I was with some of my military friends. Depriet was a marine. My friends, Riley and Michele Cook, were Navy. We went on liberty together out having fun clowning around with some ladies. Sometimes when you are having fun, you don't want to stop, but we had to get back to the base. Depriet was the driver. I heard that speed was a factor. He hit a bridge, and the van burst into flames. All three were killed, and I was the only one that survived. I suffered a fractured femur, fractured broken arm; first-, second-, and third-degree burns; and was also in a coma for a long period of time. Thanks for prayers from family and friends; I'm here today to tell my story.

Due to the care that was required for my fractured femur, the hospital had to put me in a full body cast to fly me from Oakland Naval Hospital in Oakland, California to Andrews Air Force Base, then transported to Bethesda Naval Hospital in Bethesda, Maryland so that my family and friends could visit. What a miserable experience it was for me on a four hour flight from California to Maryland. All I could do was look out the window at the clouds. But, it was worth enduring to be with my family.

It was early one morning in October 1967, after being honorably discharged from the Navy while pursuing employment. I looked in the Washington Post newspaper "Want" ad and noticed that McBride store located in Northeast Washington, DC had an opening for a furniture salesman. Unfortunately, or fortunately I didn't get the job. However, I only had enough money to catch the bus home.

At that time, my family and I lived on the 1400 block of Varnum Street, NW in Washington, DC. When the bus reached the 1300 block of H Street, NE, I saw a sign in the window of Calvinade Beauty School which read, "Veterans Enroll Now".

I remembered what my dad had suggested so I got off the bus. I also thought this must be a sign from God. He was leading me in the right direction for a career in cosmetology. I went in and asked for the Director and inquired about the study of Cosmetology and the acceptance of veterans.

I was determined to be the best; however, the practice and study of cosmetology was totally new for me and the idea of learning to curl hair seemed to be a difficult skill to learn. As a matter of fact, thinking back to that time, I remembered practicing the croquette curl on a medium length hair and it took me all day. However, I persevered and mastered that skill and many others including hair cutting and coloring. I had a firm resolve to be successful. I graduated from Calvinade Beauty Academy in Washington, DC in 1968.

The direction of Calvinade recommended me to Johnson Product Company in Chicago, IL. A company educating hairdressers on the use of its products. Back in 1977, Johnson Products was famous for Ultra Shea Gentle Treatment hair care products for the African American community. They were the first African American company to be listed on the New York Stock Exchange. I worked at several local salons before opening my own salon called Lorenzo's of Halifax Hair Designs. I'm a certified instructor with over fifty-three years of experience. I decided to write an educational book on the business of hair stylist and designs which also included how to sell and promote the business side of cosmetology and how the guests can determine if they received the proper service.

Lorenzo's of Halifax was a popular salon I owned and operated in the District of Columbia for ten years. I also was the manager of Hair Designers Plus in Hyattsville, Maryland for ten years. My other interest also included writing poetry. One of my poems was well received by President Barack Obama entitled "Tomorrow, Tomorrow, Tomorrow". I also enjoy painting landscapes and abstract art. I'm the orator on the album called "The Vision" produced by the Virginia Sons of Harmony. On that album I recited a narration entitled "Free At Last" which was my rendition of Dr. Martin Luther King's speech "I Have A Dream."

CPSIA information can be obtained
at www.ICGtesting.com
Printed in the USA
LVHW070445280721
693914LV00008B/477

9 781638 440451